Suddenly Caregiver

Now What?

When The Unexpected Happens
Know Your Options

❦

Melanie Koch

Copyright © 2021 by **Melanie Koch**

All rights reserved. No part of this publication may be reproduced, distributed or transmitted in any form or by any means, without prior written permission.

Published in Missouri (United States of America)

Publisher's Note: Whether you are currently a caregiver or not, my goal is to encourage you by sharing what I found helpful as a caregiver. Perhaps this book will create questions in your mind to help you get discussion going with your family. I don't have a medical degree—I am writing this based on my personal experience as a caregiver.

Book Layout © 2017 BookDesignTemplates.com
Book Editing and Formatting by Jeanne Felfe

ISBN 9798592402517 (paperback)

Disclaimer

Whether you are currently a caregiver or not, my goal is to encourage you by sharing what I found helpful as a caregiver.

Perhaps this book will create questions in your mind to help you get discussion going with your family.

I don't have a medical degree—I am writing this based on my personal experience as a caregiver.

Blessings, Melanie

Contents

Introduction 1

Breathe 7

Have a Plan 11

Learn Your Resources 19

Home Health Company 23

Division of Aging 27

Helpers & Institutional Living 29

Safety Concerns 35

Document Everything 41

Quick-Glance-Medical 45

Quick-Glance-Medical (EXAMPLE) ... 47

Out-of-Pocket Costs 49

Legal Issues 53

Disability Parking 57

Durable Medical Equipment—DME .. 59

Dealing with Dementia 63

Care Hugs	71
Quick-Glance-Medical Form	75
Acknowledgements	77
About the Author	79

Introduction

Just like that, suddenly and with no warning, my life changed forever. One day things were status quo and the next day Oscar needed to be monitored 24/7. But how many of us can just stop everything and become that caregiver? Since I was already on vacation that week, I decided to stay with Oscar. I pondered and prayed, "God, if you want me to quit my job and stay with Oscar, please let me know for sure."

I called my boss and explained that I was going to need to take an immediate FMLA (Family and Medical Leave Act) and would be able to give two weeks' notice if it looked like I was going to end up quitting my job. After two or three days, I knew I would be his 24/7 caregiver. I contacted my boss and explained that I was giving my notice, and we agreed on my immediate termination from the company. This was actually a simple decision for me. I felt peace about it the whole time.

FMLA provides certain employees with up to 12 weeks of unpaid, job-protected leave per year. It also requires that group health benefits be maintained during the leave. If you need to take FMLA, you should check with your human resources department to find out what you are eligible for. I don't know all the rules, but at one time, I took FMLA in small increments and then later took more as needed.

If you are dealing with an aging parent or spouse, love and respect have to be part of the mix of caring for them, not just the medical side. Just because they can't take care of themselves doesn't mean they should lose respect. If it's a parent, be sure to remind them of that in positive ways. For instance, when you are having to use tough love and implementing things they don't want to do, rather than criticize them, reinforce the respect by calling them Mom or Dad. Or say things like, "Dad, I know you don't want to and I want you to know that I don't necessarily like it either but it has to be this way." The same for spouses. Be sure to remind them they are your spouse and that you love them. Say things like, "I'm so glad we got married, I'm so glad you are my wife/husband." They may not always respond in a positive way. They may even say things like, "If you loved me you wouldn't be doing this to me." Try to remember this must have been how it felt for your parents when they were raising you and you showed resistance. Many times it's the frustration/disease speaking, not necessarily your loved one.

When you think about giving up your independence, what do you think about? What about your parents? What do you want for them? And, with that said, are your parents on the same page with you? That's a big conundrum for many. Putting your head in the sand shouldn't be an option. I know of a person who did this, and when it came time for her to be in a nursing home, her children were divided in the decision making. She did little or nothing to make the transition peaceful. Having nothing legally in place presented several challenges.

You may belong to what is called the "sandwich generation." Those who are raising children, while working and dealing with aging parents. When life happens, we don't always have a choice in the way it happens, but I feel like it is important to at least have a game plan.

I think one of the main things to remember is that your loved one didn't choose this. It was probably more frustrating for Oscar than anyone involved.

In the following pages, I want to share some basic tips I think are helpful for people to consider.

I hope in the following pages you will find things helpful either for your own situation or to share with others. What might seem like common sense to some may be an eye-opener for others.

At the end of the book is an outline summary of what I've shared. Also, I've included a sample Quick-Glance-Medical page, and a form so you can create your own. This was very helpful for me.

I hope you will be blessed and encouraged should you ever find yourself dealing with caregiving.

Breathe

I became a 24/7 caregiver without warning. One day, a dear family member—I'll call him "Oscar"—was suddenly taken to the hospital. Upon discharge from the hospital, it was apparent that Oscar shouldn't be left alone. But who would take care of him? He certainly wouldn't have gone along with assisted living—that wasn't conducive to his personality. Keeping him in his home with things as normal as possible, was the best option for him.

Oscar and I got along great, and I had enough experience in the medical field to make me the logical choice. I was at a point in my life that allowed me to do it.

If you find yourself in a similar situation, the thing I think is so important is to breathe. Take a moment and take a breath. Don't panic!

While some people have things prearranged, they might still go into a panic when it really happens to their loved one. It's fine to deal with your emotions of frustration about what will happen next, as well as the declining health of the loved one. However, I think it's best not to camp out in the feeling of despair for too long. You need your energy and clear thinking. Take a breath! Cope with the situation as well as you can and ask for help if you need it. Realize that not all those you ask for help will be there for you like you had imagined they would be. While others step up and are available beyond your wildest dreams.

Some things you have control over, some you don't. Learning to live one day at a time, one moment at a time, can really alleviate stress. Also, I considered it an honor to care for Oscar. I think a positive attitude helps you cope a little better than if you feel overburdened. Stay focused on all the positives.

Find the coping skills that work best for you! For me, it was feeling this was an honor given to me to love on my person that I was the caregiver for. I wanted to give him the best days, for the rest of his days. My personal goal was to keep him out of a nursing home.

Have a Plan

Many people think they have plenty of time to consider options. Some don't plan at all. They wing it and go with the flow. Seems for some, things work out regardless of whether they planned it or just went with the flow. Whatever camp you find yourself in, it truly is worth considering what you would do if the situation arose.

If you already have all your ducks in a row regarding extended care options, great! You should periodically review your plan—perhaps annually depending on your situation.

Let me give an example of why you should review your current plan. I knew a family with three sons and two daughters. The parents had everything set up in the two daughters' names. When the father died, the mother didn't make any updates. One of the sons had preceded both parents in death. Eventually, one of the daughters died. No one thought to update the information. Then another son died. Later, the second daughter died and in less than two weeks, the mother also died. The remaining son was left to finalize his mother's estate. Not only was the son dealing with the grief of his sister and mother, he now was responsible for the mother's estate. Without being named on any of the legal documents, he had to obtain a lawyer. He had to obtain birth and death certificates of all of his siblings to prove he was the sole heir. I'm sure you can see how this situation could have been alleviated if they had monitored their estate plans. Even if the estate is small, having a plan with the appropriate individuals on all accounts is crucial.

If you have never considered making final arrangements, now would be a good time to do so. Many people feel they are too young and will get around to it eventually. Old age is not a guarantee. It's best to make the arrangements while things are simpler rather than when things are going crazy. One less thing to worry about is such a blessing during a time/crisis such as this.

At the time of this writing, I knew a family going through some tough decisions. The mother refused to delegate any of her grown children as legal guardian or medical Power of Attorney (POA). One of the children had tried over the years to get her to do so. The mother went into a rehab facility and was possibly going to become a long-term resident. None of her children could legally do anything with her house, car, or belongings. The siblings weren't all on the same page, which complicated things even more. If there had been legal documents establishing the mother's desires, it would have resolved a lot of tension between the siblings. It was already hard enough watching her decline. The facility tried to work with her to get her to sign things, but she refused. She felt like she would be giving up her independence. I don't feel that this is a rare situation.

It finally became necessary for the mother to become a long-term resident of the nursing home. Two of her children were in agreement, but the third child (who lived out of state) wasn't. It appeared that one of the children was experiencing a classic example of denial. This grown man was having trouble accepting the fact that his mother was declining to the point of needing 24/7 care. He thought more could be done and that the other two siblings should have tried harder to help. This brought division and hurt between the siblings. At a time when the focus should have been strictly on the mother, the siblings were dealing with raw emotions of their own. If the mother had at least had things legalized before this started happening, it would have alleviated a lot of stress. Not only were the siblings dealing with the health issues of their mother, they now were faced with what to do with her house and possessions. Again, they could not agree.

In another scenario, I knew a man who had been married and divorced. He had lived with a woman for over twelve years, when with little warning, he was suddenly hospitalized and on life support. He had two adult children. When the doctors felt they had exhausted all possibilities for him to recover, a decision had to be made. The live-in girlfriend wanted to make the decision, but unfortunately he had never made any legal arrangements of any kind. The doctor appointed his oldest child to make the decision. While the two children agreed on turning off the life support, the girlfriend wasn't ready. After days of anguish, the decision was finally made to disconnect all life support and let him go.

Hospitals see this scenario more than they should. It's very uncomfortable for the hospital staff, not to mention how stressful it is to the family at such a sad time.

Besides not having legal medical plans, he also didn't have any legal financial plans. The house payment was more than the girlfriend could manage, so she had to move out. His grown children couldn't afford the house payments, so the house had to go into foreclosure.

These are things that people might not think of, or think they'll someday get around to it.

I have watched families almost torn apart over these kinds of things. My hope in writing this book is to encourage people to stop and think long range and not put things off thinking there is always tomorrow.

Personally, I think it's good if one of the executors is a non-family member. Oftentimes, family members get emotional and things don't always flow smoothly. Of course, this is a personal preference.

Whoever the executor or POA is, they should have a copy of the documents. Some facilities will require proof of POA rather than someone's word. It's not a bad idea to take a copy with you to doctors' offices and have the document(s) put it in the person's chart. Hospitals can also put them on file for future reference.

I don't think adults are ever too young to take care of these things. Parents should consider what would happen to their minor children if something tragic happened and they weren't able to care for them. I'm not going to get into this topic, just putting it out there for consideration.

Learn Your Resources

Check with your local ambulance district to learn what resources are available to you. In this section, I outline some of the services I found available in my district.

You can check with your local ambulance department to see if they have a program such as Citizen's Assist. Prior to this experience, I didn't realize the ambulance district where I was a caregiver had a separate telephone number for a program called "Citizen's Assist." I didn't even know it existed until the ambulance personnel told me. It was quite useful to know. Citizen's Assist would come help put your loved one in the car for you to take them somewhere and then you could call them upon return and they'd come back and help bring the person into the house.

Citizen's Assist was truly a blessing when Oscar became a fall risk. Especially when it was very cold, his legs would sometimes just give out. I wasn't strong enough to handle him. Like they told me, they'd rather help than to have to come back with him on the ground with a broken hip or worse.

When he was on oxygen, they would disconnect the concentrator in the house and hook up the tank and get him situated in the car. This was nice.

They also would come lift Oscar if he couldn't get up out of a chair or off the floor. They would do a triage and if he was stable and didn't need transport to the hospital, they'd be on their way.

Oscar was very weak after a hospitalization and had trouble getting out of his swivel recliner (which ended up being replaced with a lift chair) and I had to call Citizen's Assist to help me with him. He didn't make it to the bathroom and so they stood him up and held him while I cleaned him up. They even assisted in helping change his clothing. They were such a Godsend.

They also told me about a program called Rapid Access Program. This program could be very helpful to anyone, whether a caregiver or not. In the district where I served, they can install a keypad for $25, one-time fee. They have the combination and if you need to call for help and can't get to the door, they can enter your house without breaking down your door. The EMS personnel told me that if they have to come to the house, it's already a bad day, but if they have to break the door down, it's an even worse day. Not only do you have to deal with the original emergency, you have to figure out how to secure the house at the same time. Since Oscar was never left alone, I didn't utilize the keypad, but it was nice of them to explain it to me.

I love how supportive the EMS were. They were of course taking care of the patient, but they also understand the importance of taking care of the caregiver. Sometimes their encouraging words to me were what made the difference in a tough situation.

Home Health Company

Many people don't realize they can choose which company they want to use. Some doctors only refer to a specific company. Some doctors will ask you which one you would like to use—Oscar's doctor actually asked. I wanted a company that had everything under the same umbrella for continuity of care for Oscar as well as myself as a caregiver. A company that I knew of partnered with an Adult Day Care. The company I chose was awesome to work with—they were truly there for us.

A lot of people don't know how this works until they need one. Home Health must be ordered by a doctor. Most insurances cover home health. There are criteria/guidelines that are set up. The company will pre-certify with the insurance company and then explain all of your options and coverage for your particular insurance. Besides nursing, they will explain if the patient meets criteria for physical therapy, occupational therapy, bath aide, etc.

Once we no longer met criteria for the bath aide, I used the Private Services division for that. It was helpful to have the same person attending to his bathing needs, especially as the dementia started. The bath aide had a connection with Oscar, and I didn't want to change that. Continuity of care was very important to me.

Adult Day Care is typically a fee-for-service, meaning you pay out-of-pocket. Adult day care is much like child day care. You drop your loved one off and pick them up at designated times. The company will have you complete a medical assessment for them and in our case, the doctor had to sign off on it. They not only offered watching and feeding the patient, they had additional services you could pay for such as bathing assistance, etc.

Oscar didn't utilize this service, but I know a family member who did. This was a tremendous blessing for the family who did utilize the Adult Day Care. The spouse was able to run errands and have some me-time, knowing her spouse was being well taken care of.

Private Services cover a wide variety of things. It can be respite care—someone coming to sit with the patient while you go to the doctor yourself, or just need a breather/get away. They also have bath aide assistance, house cleaning assistance, etc. This was a fee-for-service. We only needed to utilize private services for the bath aide.

Hospice is typically covered by insurance. The company should be able to tell you what your benefits are. Hospice can be utilized either in your loved one's home or a nursing home facility. A social worker can assist in nursing home placement if it is needed. If the person is going to have hospice at home, they also assist in that. Hospice isn't like it was many years ago. It used to be when someone went on hospice, they were going to die and that was all there was to it. Now, there are many levels of hospice care, including palliative care. Some people actually come off of hospice, and not by means of death. The company representative should be able to go over all the options with you. The company we worked with (we didn't end up using hospice) had a chaplain, massage therapy, music therapy, and more available.

I felt like having one company that had all the resources I needed or might need was the best option.

Division of Aging

You can check for a Division of Aging in your area. They are a government agency that assists on various levels. They will check your income and insurance and then let you know what you are approved for. Some people qualify for Meals on Wheels at no cost to them. A lot depends upon your income.

Oscar was approved for adult diapers and nutrition supplements. They had two options available for us. We could either let them send us what they had available and deliver it to the home, or I could purchase and be reimbursed. I did my homework and found that I could do better purchasing what I needed and turning in the receipts for reimbursement. I was able to get more bang for my buck by doing this because I used coupons. Some would prefer not having to hassle with shopping and just let them send the stuff to your house. It was nice to have the option.

Online shopping is another resource for people today. Having home delivery whether shopping online or having a local store delivered is a convenience that many appreciate.

Helpers & Institutional Living

Some people opt to have private duty help in the home. That can be wonderful, if you can find qualified and dependable people who are available right away. You need at least two if the family members are available to participate. If you go this route, be sure to have backup available. What happens if the private duty person becomes ill, needs to take off for a doctor's appointment or a funeral, or wants a vacation?

Assisted living is an option for some people. When I toured such a facility, they told me the resident had to be able to get out of the building on their own in case of a fire. Assisted living monitors the resident. They assist in reminding them to take their medication and how much to take. They will assist in bathing, if required. Laundry is a featured service for most, if not all. Some offer activities such as tour bus trips. Most like to keep the resident active and living their best life.

Assisted living facilities are usually very eye appealing with dining room, libraries, game rooms, and other resident-focused amenities. Their goal is to make the resident content and safe while they are giving up their independence. Most, if not all, have a waiting list.

Yes, there are nursing homes. It's a good idea to select one convenient for your family and get your loved one's name on their waiting list. Don't feel locked in by this. Just because someone is on the waiting list doesn't mean they have to accept it when their name comes up. For most, entering into a nursing home comes after being discharged from a hospital and a hospital social worker coordinates the transition. The social worker coordinates with the insurance company to determine the benefits available for your loved one. Most insurance will cover the transition for a specified time period based on medical criteria. Once they no longer meet the criteria, they can be discharged to home, or become a permanent resident if they aren't well enough to return to home. Long term care is the patient's financial responsibility. The costs add up so quickly. Most of the people I know have to pay at least $6,000 a month, if not more. Often people run out of money and end up going on Medicaid. Again, social workers assist with this.

If your loved one is a Veteran, there are Veteran nursing homes. You need to apply ahead of time. Contact the Veteran's Administration and obtain an application. The veteran or legal custodian has to complete and submit the form. The form requires detailed medical information, preference of locations available in the area, and the doctor's signature.

Someone I knew was on the waiting list for a Veteran's Home. When he no longer met insurance criteria to remain in hospital, the facility of choice didn't have any beds available. The social worker found some other nursing homes with allotted Veteran beds available. The patient could transition to that facility and receive his Veteran benefits. Hospital social workers are very well versed in the ins and outs of nursing home availability and requirements for admission.

Nursing homes have upped their game and try to make facilities more eye appealing. Activity directors strive to keep the residents engaged, but face it, not all people want to participate. It's definitely a lifestyle change. Suddenly, you have people telling you what your schedule is rather than being in charge of your life.

Some residents in nursing homes refuse to participate. They sit in their rooms and many think they are there just biding their time until they die. I know people who have referred to their placement in a nursing home as being in prison or stuck in a dungeon. It's important to try to help them understand it's not a punishment. It's because they require good care and you're unable to provide for their needs. Try to find a way to encourage them in making this transition. Consider what you would want.

There is the issue of cost. Facilities aren't cheap. And, if your loved one ends up needing memory care, that can add to the cost. These are things to consider ahead of time to make for a smoother transition.

Whichever route you end up taking, when you become the caregiver, you also become the patient advocate. It's important to follow-up on things. You need to check in with facilities and not just assume things are going well. Many times, your loved one will tell you one thing while the staff tells you something else. You need to learn how to discern who is correct. You don't want your loved one thinking you don't believe them or don't care. And at the same time, you don't want the facility thinking you don't trust them or that you think they are lying. I suggest getting acquainted with the facility staff. Building a rapport by checking in often, whether by telephone or visits, enhances the relationship with the family and the facility. The facility actually becomes an extended family. Letting the staff know you appreciate them is a relationship builder. Sending thank you cards to acknowledge people who are working with not only your family member but many others encourages them.

Safety Concerns

Home health sent an Occupational Therapist (OT) to the home to access safety. The OT made recommendations and then came back later to reevaluate. Oscar was a fall risk, so the OT was glad there were no throw rugs on the floors. Rugs that slip can be a hazard for someone who has balance issues.

One thing the OT noted was there were no grab bars in the walk-in shower. She suggested that if we didn't want to have permanent grab bars installed, we could purchase suction ones and place them in the shower. I purchased the suction grab bars and had the bath aide assist in the proper placement for Oscar's height. From personal experience, it's good to check to be sure the suction hasn't loosened before using each time. If I noticed the tabs had flipped up, I knew they needed to be secured again.

OT was happy to see that Oscar's kitchen chair had arms on it, making it easier for him in transitioning from sitting to standing. What seems like a simple thing really can be an important factor.

OT might also suggest grab bars around the toilet area. Some bedside commodes can actually be placed over the top of the existing toilet, and they have the grab handles to push up with.

Oscar's home needed some handrails installed outside. The one he had on his deck wasn't the best solution for him. I called around trying to find someone who could do the job quickly and cost effectively. One of the places I called suggested a particular church group, so I contacted them.

The Hammer Heads (a church-based group) installed rails for safety on an already existing deck. This particular group quoted that they only charge for supplies and not labor. This was a tremendous blessing. Check with local churches to find out if there are options in your neighborhood. A lot of people want the opportunity to help others, they just don't know the opportunity exists until someone tells them. Reach out and ask.

Walkers and wheelchairs need extra clearance. You may have to rearrange furniture to accommodate for this. If the loved one has dementia, be mindful of this when moving things. You want to keep things as normal as possible. Change can be hard on a person with dementia.

Many homes have open stairwells. This is a concern for some people, especially for a person who is a fall risk. Baby gates are often used. If you use a stair lift, gates might not work for that. OT suggested a chair lift for the stairs, but since Oscar no longer went to the basement, there was no need to pay all that money for one.

Safety proofing the home is much like baby proofing. With an adult, keep in mind they may not like the modifications you are putting into place. Especially if they have dementia, they can even become defensive because they might not understand, or they don't want to accept they are getting feeble. Try to think of positive ways to implement the changes and still show respect to one you are caring for.

Wandering off, thankfully, wasn't an issue with Oscar. However, it is a concern. Some homes already have alarm systems that can be set so that if your loved one starts to leave the house unattended, it signals you. If the house already has an alarm system, you might want to change the code. That might be the one thing your love one actually remembers. There are many options available. Discussing them with the home health providers is often helpful, as well as doing your own research. I recommend not discussing this in front of the person you are caring for. You might think they don't comprehend what you are saying, but you might be surprised when they are climbing on a chair to disengage the alarm on the door.

This is not an exhaustive list of safety precautions. Each situation is unique. The OT can be very helpful in this area.

Document Everything

I can't stress strongly enough the importance of documentation. Miscommunication happens no matter how careful we are, but documentation can cut way back on that. In my opinion, it's crucial!

Because Oscar was a diabetic, he had to take insulin with meals. His blood sugar had to be checked before each meal. I calculated the number of carbs per meal and dosed the insulin based on a chart provided by the doctor. Oscar had been documenting this before he needed a caregiver.

I'm not a computer savvy person, so I did it the old fashion way—pen and paper. I recorded the name and dose of medication and the times I gave each. Be sure to include over-the-counter medications such as vitamins and supplements as well.

Especially if a patient is on pain medication, it's also important to keep track of bowel movements. Some medications cause constipation. You don't want to give laxatives if not needed.

If EMS assistance was needed, I also documented the visit and reason for the visit. As well as Emergency Room visits. Basically, it was a journal of the journey.

It's extremely important to document so you can be as error proof as humanly possible. When EMS comes or you go to ER, it's great to know this information to assist in the care your loved one receives. In the middle of a crisis, you might not remember the last time they took a particular medication. Overdosing is not a good thing.

If you share caregiver responsibilities, documentation is imperative. Suppose the patient is on a routine regimen that both caregivers know. However, on a particular day, the patient didn't take the dose of medication at the usual time, for whatever reason, and actually took it a few hours later. At the changing of the guard, you don't think to relay that information. If the next caregiver gives the patient medication at usual time, you could have a real problem.

If there are concerns or drastic changes, it's always good to document. What might seem like no big deal to you might actually be a critical sign to a medical professional. Let the medical team decide. For instance, if you notice your loved one taking more naps and longer naps than usual, you might want to document it and discuss it with the doctor. Even changes in eating habits. Of course, some days we are hungrier than others, but if there is a big change or a loss of appetite, it should be discussed with your medical provider.

Documenting doesn't have to be spreadsheets or elaborate, it just needs to be done orderly and consistently.

Quick-Glance-Medical

The Quick-Glance-Medical sheet is my passion. I can't emphasize enough how beneficial this is. I was praised by ERs, doctor's offices, EMS, and even hospitals for this. One hospital pharmacist came into Oscar's room to tell me how much she appreciated how I not only listed his allergies, but what his reactions were—she said this helped tremendously.

I have even created one for my own medical records. This is a vital tool everyone should have, whether they are a caregiver or not. It helps you keep your medical records clean and accurate.

On the next page you'll find an example of the Quick-Glance-Medical documentation I used for Oscar. At the end of the book, you'll find a blank form. You are welcome to print it for your use.

Quick-Glance-Medical (EXAMPLE)

Patient's LEGAL Name_____
(Goes by "_____")
Date of Birth

Allergies: Lisinopril (throat tightness), Mucinex DM (HTN), Augmentin XR (thrush), Wool (rash)

Medications:

    Humalog insulin—sliding scale
    Lantus insulin—16 units at breakfast
        & 7 units at hs
    Furosemide 20 mg qod
    Isosorbide Mononitrate 30 mg q d
    Bayer Low Dose Aspirin
    Avodart 0.5 mg
    Centrum Silver Multivitamin
    Pantoprazole 40 mg BID
    D3 2000 i.u.
    Amiodarone
    Spiriva Respimat 2 puffs q am
    Ventolin Inhaler PRN

Medical Conditions:

    Brittle IDDM
    Mild CHF—Edema
    A-Fib (2015)

Bradycardia
ASHD (Coronary Atherosclerosis)
COPD
Emphysema
BPH
Memory Loss – Diabetes Dementia
Orthostatic Hypotension
Benign Hypertension
Severe Grade D Esophagitis (January 6, 2015)
Severe Osteoporosis (High risk of fx) Fall Risk
Pelvic Fx 1-14-15
L4 Fx 2-13-15
Aspiration Pneumonia (January 2015)

Previous Conditions:
Kyphoplasty L2 (3-13-14)
Kyphoplasty L1 (9-2009)
Squamous Cell (leg and arms)
Cataract Surgery (both eyes)
Gallbladder removed (1994)
Throat Cancer (1993)

Out-of-Pocket Costs

Not everything is covered by insurance—these costs are known as "out of pocket." These might include prescriptions, over the counter items, or private duty services. Be sure to keep receipts and records of all of these expenses.

Sometimes we can't go to multiple pharmacies because of the time involved. But if at all possible, call around and find out the prices before the doctor sends out a prescription. Some wholesale clubs allow non-members to utilize their pharmacy. Because they are a wholesale, they can often get you better deals. The local pharmacy we used suggested this to me when Oscar was prescribed a medication not covered by his insurance. Going to a wholesale club saved approximately $70 per month. Some pharmacies will actually contact the current pharmacy and have the script transferred to them.

A drive-thru pharmacy is especially helpful if your loved one has to be in the car with you, perhaps on the way home from the hospital. It isn't safe to leave some patients alone in a vehicle while you run in to pick up a script. Sometimes the weather isn't good for that either. Also, patients that are a fall risk are safer if you can go through the drive-thru. This was the case for us.

Paying for private duty services was another out-of-pocket expense for Oscar. Like previously mentioned, I utilized the bath aide from home health as a private duty service for continuity of care for Oscar. Keep receipts of those payments as well.

Incontinence products can become a very costly out-of-pocket expense. This can include adult diapers, underpads for a person to sit on or have under them in bed, etc. There are incontinence cleaners and lotions that most likely aren't covered by any insurance.

When Oscar had a wound that was being treated by home health, the insurance covered the wound care supplies, such as bandages and creams. However, after he was discharged from home health and still need continuing wound care, the costs were his responsibility.

The lift chair was another out-of-pocket expense. Lift chairs serve a wonderful purpose but a word of caution—monitor a loved one with dementia to be sure they understand how the remote works. One day Oscar was in the recliner lift chair with his legs elevated—per doctor's instructions—and decided to get up. Unable to comprehend the remote, he couldn't figure out how to get the leg rest to go down. I walked into the room just in time to see him trying to climb out of the chair. The chair was light weight and could have easily tipped over—thankfully it didn't.

The costs can really add up. So again, save all receipts. Sometimes you spend more on over the counter items than you realize until you start tracking it. This can come in handy during tax time. They can be thrown away later if not needed.

Legal Issues

Many people today are on top of their game with the legal issues. However, sometimes we think we have it all figured out ahead of time only to find out we missed a few things. If you already have things set up, do a review.

Find out who can pay bills for your loved one if they are unable to do so. Check with the bank regarding who can sign the checks if your loved one isn't able.

Be sure you are included on the HIPAA forms in all the medical facilities—it will save frustration. Some places won't even let you discuss the bills or make payments if you're not listed on the HIPAA.

It's crucial to have a Power of Attorney (POA). A POA is a legal document authorizing a person or persons to carry out your desires—financial and medical—when you are incapable of doing so. These can be two separate documents. Sometimes the financial POA agent isn't the same person as the medical POA agent.

HIPAA and POA are not the same thing. For example, recently a person was in a nursing home and had all her children listed on the HIPAA forms. She finally decided to sign a medical durable POA. When one of her children called to check on her, they were told they could no longer discuss the patient's care because a POA had been signed. The staff was incorrect. The misunderstanding was later cleared up. During the time of getting this miscommunication rectified, there was a lot of stress on the family.

A durable POA continues indefinitely after the point when you're legally not able to make your own decisions. A hospital social services department can direct you in obtaining this or you can go through an attorney.

Some durable POA are very specific. Oscar's was quite detailed. The legal forms were obtained from hospital social services. Oscar filled them out in the presence of the social service department and two notaries signed them. His POA specified how he wanted things handled if he wasn't capable of making a medical decision—things such as if he should need life giving machines or even antibiotics with no prognosis of survival, and how many doctors he wanted consulted on a life-giving decision, etc. By having this detailed document, his POA was responsible for executing his desires. The ambulance people told me to be sure to have it available every time they came in so I could show it to them if need be.

Be sure the POA is kept current. If you only have one POA agent listed, you might consider adding a second person as a backup should the primary person not be available.

Remember, if a POA isn't in place, social workers at hospitals and nursing homes have access to the forms. They need to be signed and notarized. You don't have to go through an attorney, so don't let the thought of legal fees keep you from taking care of this.

Get all of this prepared while the patient is of sound mind. Should the patient slip into dementia, you might need to have them declared incompetent, and going through a court is emotionally difficult in these situations. Planning ahead can help in so many ways.

Disability Parking

Some people qualify to utilize disability license plates. I chose to get the tag that you can hang in your car. By having the tag, if more than one person transports your loved one, you can switch the tag back and forth between drivers and vehicles.

To obtain a disability parking tag or license plate, a doctor must sign off on the form. Contact your local driver's license bureau and find out their policy.

After Oscar passed away, I put the tag away with his things and didn't think about it. Later, when a renewal notice came, it stated that it was illegal not to return the tag. I had to get his things out and check for it, hoping I hadn't shredded it. Fortunately, I did have it and was able to return it to the license bureau.

Durable Medical Equipment—DME

If you know the resources before you need them, you can save money. Saving money is really important because there are a lot of things that aren't covered by insurance benefits.

Some insurance companies will cover a wheelchair, but not a wheelchair and a walker. Some will cover a walker but not a wheelchair too.

If you need to have a hospital bed set up in the home, check with your insurance company to see if there is any coverage for one. A medical supply company can guide in making arrangements for a bed in the home. Some pay a rental fee and once the bed is no longer needed, the company comes and picks it up.

Bedside commodes are also considered DME and most likely have to be paid out-of-pocket.

There are places that take in used DME and sanitize the items and offer them to people free or at discounted prices. Knowing this ahead of time can help set your mind at ease.

If you utilize used equipment such as a walker, be sure it's adjustable and at the proper height for your loved one. Same goes for canes. Grandpa's cane might not work for Grandma—have a professional help you for proper height. Some physical therapists prefer using a four prong cane, but don't feel they are correct for every situation. Let the professionals decide for you.

A Rollator is like a walker but has a drop-down seat. Again, check with the therapist to be sure it's the right assist for your loved one.

Again, if you end up paying out-of-pocket for any DME, keep your receipt. If you have time and energy, journaling the date and costs of out-of-pocket expenses can help you reference it easily.

Dealing with Dementia

One thing I've learned about dementia throughout my life is that the patient isn't trying to give you a hard time, they are *having* a hard time. They are probably more frustrated than you are. Imagine knowing that your mind is slipping away and you can't do anything to stop it. Try keeping that in mind.

Another thing I tried to always remember was to love them, no matter. No regrets! In their frustration, they may yell at you, may even curse you, but again, it's the disease. Always, always, always try to show them respect. Remember, they are an adult. Love them like a toddler, but respect them as an adult. One frustration that many face is the loss of control. They may even feel a loss of purpose. Try to express how important they are to you, whether they are your parent, grandparent, spouse, or whatever your relationship is with them. Perhaps you can tell them how much you enjoy just spending time with them.

Whenever possible, give them options, not commands. When there are things they are difficult about, such as bathing and/or changing clothes, learn to work with that, not fight with them. For instance, if they feel like they haven't done anything to get their clothes dirty and don't want to put on fresh clothes, maybe you can do a load of laundry that would include that piece of clothing and ask them if you can have it to complete your load. In my case, it worked. Oscar wanted to be accommodating, most of the time.

Sometimes I would just fix his meals. Eventually, I had to do the dosing of the medications and blood sugar monitoring. However, on good days, I could ask him what he preferred. Since I mentioned "good days," that brings up something else. With dementia patients, sometimes, they seem so lost and other times, they seem with it and it's like they are back to normal. Some say they are messing with you, playing mind games, but I disagree. I think their minds fade in and out in the process of slipping into the next stages. It seems to be a progressive disease for most people I've been associated with.

Don't argue with a dementia patient. Oscar's favorite ball team was in first place and had won twelve games in a row and lost a game. It upset him and he said they were a bad team and needed to work on their game. I mentioned they were in first place and had won twelve in a row. It agitated him, so I dropped it. He was focused on the current loss. I suggested changing the channel and watching something else and fortunately, that worked.

Try to enjoy your time together. There were times we would just sit together, and to make him feel more secure, I would pat him on his leg, or hold his hand. This was not time wasted. A comforting touch can mean so much, just like you would do for a frightened baby or child. The ministry of presence is very powerful.

One thing I realized is not to quiz your loved one. Instead of asking questions like "do you remember?" start conversations and let them participate. It can help you figure out where they are mentally at the moment. Asking someone if they remember when they know they are forgetting and losing their mental acuity, can exacerbate their frustration.

You may think you are trying to keep their mind active and memory skills working, but don't continually ask them if they remember such-and-such. Oscar loved music and knew a lot of songs. As he started progressing with the dementia, he couldn't always remember lyrics. Rather than asking him words to songs, sometimes I would just start singing and he would chime in. If I didn't know all the words, I'd say that I didn't know any more of it, and sometimes he could continue the song.

When they can't find their words, help them. If they are trying to tell you something and are getting frustrated because they can't come up with the words, try to help fill in the blanks for them. Sometimes that works, sometimes it doesn't. Try to put yourself in their shoes and imagine what they must be feeling. I think it's much like when a child is first learning words and can't always come up with the right word right away. This is almost like reverse.

Try to let them be part of decision making as much as possible. I would ask Oscar what he wanted to eat and sometimes he would tell me—other times, he just didn't know. When he didn't know, I'd suggest something and for the most part, he was agreeable with my suggestion.

When you have to override their decisions, try not to take it personal if they lash out at you. They may have a doctor's appointment and not want to go. They might get really agitated if you insist. If it's a routine follow-up, call the office and see if you can reschedule. Most doctor's offices will work with you when they know you are dealing with dementia. If it's one they really need to go to, you might have to resort to bribery. I would try to schedule Oscar's appointments around his eating and insulin times. A lot of times we would be headed back from the appointment in time to drive thru and bring home a meal he enjoyed.

Sometimes Oscar would ask me about people in his family. One day he asked about his sister. She had been dead for several years and I wasn't quite sure how he would handle it. But I just told him she passed away and he was okay with that. I didn't want to say, "I can't believe you don't remember that she died." That would serve no purpose. Try to be mindful of these things.

Always reinforce your love for the patient. I suggest when dealing with dementia, treat them with the patience you would a baby, when at all possible. It can get intense when they have to do something they don't want to, and they say hateful things to you. Again, remind yourself, it's not them but the disease that is speaking.

Sometimes they might say things like, "You'd be better off if you didn't have to take care of me." With Oscar, I'd tell him, "I love being with you and I'm happy to help you." I felt like by saying I was helping him, it didn't make him feel like such a burden. Plus, it might actually make him feel like he had a little control of things if I was only helping.

Cell phone texting is an amazing tool for the caregiver. When discussing your loved one with family members, try to text things that might upset the patient rather than discussing it in front of them. Email or patient portals for doctors' offices are also a good way to communicate without the patient hearing you. Try not to discuss anything negative in front of the patient. You don't know how they will interpret what you are saying.

Care Hugs

The following are what I call care hugs because it's my way of offering a hug to a caregiver.

We may think we are prepared and still have surprises pop up. But the more we know ahead of time, the better we can handle things.

Prioritize—everything doesn't have to be done immediately. Your house doesn't have to look like a showroom. As someone once told me, "A house should be clean enough to be healthy, and dirty enough to be happy."

When the patient rests—you rest—it's OKAY!!!

Don't be too proud or too independent to ask for help (my shortcoming). I didn't want to burden others; I wanted to handle things on my own.

There are support groups for just about everything. If your loved one has specific health issues you aren't familiar with, reach out and learn more. There are so many resources available, however, during the time of caregiving, you can't always research the best resources. The patient's healthcare team is a good place to start. In many cases, they can direct you to the help you need. Don't be afraid to ask—that is what they are there for. It may be your first time caregiving, but they have been at it a while, so let them help. Home health social workers as well as hospital social workers have many resources.

I was very blessed by a great team of healthcare professionals. The doctors and home health company I used worked great together.

Spiritual Helps—as a 24/7 caregiver, I wasn't able to attend church, so I found some online services I enjoyed. Sometimes I would even drift off and have to replay them—another benefit of having that available.

If you have a particular prayer or Scripture that comforts you, such as The Serenity Prayer, have it available.

A Scripture that is still precious to me is Isaiah 26:3. Paraphrasing—He will keep those in perfect peace whose mind is stayed upon the Lord. Sometimes, I would say, "Lord, I need that peace now, my mind is on You, and I'm claiming that calming peace for myself." Or as I walked into the ER, I would be reciting the Scripture.

Be sure to eat and stay hydrated. Some caregivers forget about their own nutrition. You are important and it's vital to care for yourself as well.

Being a control person and an over thinker/planner, I emailed with several funeral homes over the years to compare pricing. I liked that email was an option so I didn't have to discuss things in front of Oscar. If your loved one is a Veteran, be sure to state that. Even if they aren't buried at a National Cemetery, they will qualify for certain benefits. The funeral home will be able to assist with covered benefits based on the person's DD214—the Discharge from Active Duty certificate.

Again, let me say, I was honored to be Oscar's caregiver. It was my last chance to love on him before he slipped into eternity. I'm glad I made the best of it. And yes, it was difficult at times. And yes, he hurt my feelings sometimes, but I would remind myself it wasn't really him.

If you find yourself caregiving, **love on them**!

Quick-Glance-Medical Form

LEGAL Name: _____

Goes by: _____

Date of Birth: _____ Date Document Updated: _____

Allergies—Medication / Substance   Reaction

_____   _____
_____   _____
_____   _____
_____   _____
_____   _____

Medications   Dosage

_____   _____
_____   _____
_____   _____
_____   _____
_____   _____
_____   _____

Current Medical Conditions: Date of Onset

_____   _____
_____   _____
_____   _____
_____   _____
_____   _____

Previous Conditions: Date

_____   _____
_____   _____
_____   _____
_____   _____
_____   _____

Acknowledgements

I thank God for assigning me the honor of being a caregiver. I give Him credit for the strength He gave me to fulfill the role. I appreciate His favor in connecting me with the medical personnel that worked along with me. Words can never express my gratitude.

A great big thank you to Jeanne Felfe, author and President of Saturday Writers in St. Peters, Missouri. Jeanne's experience, insights, and edits made this book come to fruition. Thank you Jeanne for encouraging me along the way.

Carol, my dear, dear friend who journeyed the journey with me while I was a 24/7 caregiver. For over three years I relied on her for almost daily telephone calls. Thank you for driving two hours to bring a sturdy bench for Oscar to use outdoors when I had no way to shop for one. I could never repay you for all the kindness and support you showed.

Mitchell, thank you for sitting with Oscar when I had to go to the doctor. Oscar never wanted to have a sitter but Mitchell hung out with him and they had men time together. It certainly made it easier for me to relax knowing he was comfortable with you. And for being the fix-it man when home repairs were needed. You saved Oscar a lot of money.

M. Rose Callahan—cover design. Thank you Rose for taking my idea and implementing it.

About the Author

Melanie Koch is an encourager. By sharing both good and bad experiences she demonstrates there is always something to be thankful for.

Melanie's desire is to inspire compassion and an attitude of gratitude while dealing with difficult circumstances.

As a beginning writer, she is simplistic with a passion to share with others something she believes in.

Made in the USA
Middletown, DE
21 April 2022